The World of Composers

Tchaikovsky

Greta Cencetti

PETER BEDRICK BOOKS

McGraw-Hill
Children's Publishing

A Division of The **McGraw·Hill** Companies

This edition published in the United States in 2002 by
Peter Bedrick Books, an imprint of
McGraw-Hill Children's Publishing,
A Division of The McGraw-Hill Companies
8787 Orion Place
Columbus, Ohio 43240

www.MHkids.com

ISBN 1-58845-472-X

Library of Congress Cataloging-in-Publication Data

Cencetti, Greta.
Tchaikovsky / Greta Cencetti.
p. cm. -- (The world of composers)
Summary: An introduction to the life and musical career
of the nineteenth-century Russian composer.
ISBN 1-58845-472-X
1. Tchaikovsky, Peter Ilich, 1840-1893--Juvenile literature. 2. Composers—Russia—
Biography—Juvenile literature. [1. Tchaikovsky, Peter Ilich, 1840-1893.
2. Composers.] I. Title. II. Series.

ML3930.C4 C46 2002
780'.92--dc21
[B]
2001052538

© 2002 Ta Chien Publishing Co., Ltd.
© 2002 Studio Mouse

10 9 8 7 6 5 4 3 2 1 CHRT 06 05 04 03 02

Printed in China.

The World of Composers

Tchaikovsky

Greta Cencetti

PETER BEDRICK BOOKS

Contents

Chapter 1
A Sensitive Child

Peter Ilich Tchaikovsky (pronounced chy-KAWF-skee) was born on May 7, 1840, in the village of Votkinsk, in Russia. Tchaikovsky's father, Ilya, was an engineer, and his mother, Aleksandra, was a pianist.

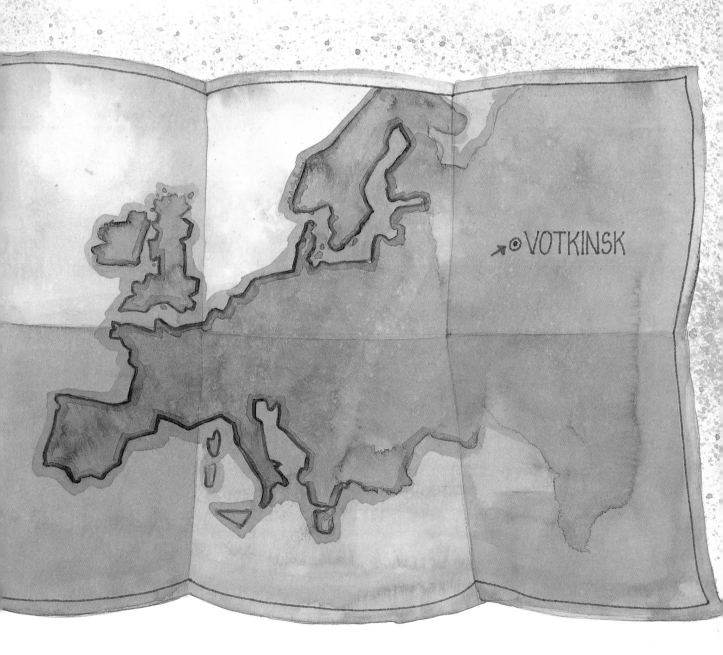

Young Peter was a described as a handsome boy, but he was not very strong. Because he was frail, his family took great care in raising him. He was the second son of a large family. He was a sensitive boy, who often seemed to be quite nervous. It did not take much to upset him.

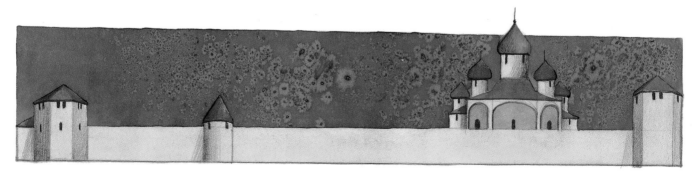

1848

As a young boy, Tchaikovsky listened to his mother playing the piano. Music soon became the center of his life. His family members noticed that when he was seated at a table, he moved his fingers over it as though it were a piano.

When Peter was only five, his mother and father asked a woman named Fanny Durbach to teach him to play the piano. He learned quickly, and the piano would become his companion for life.

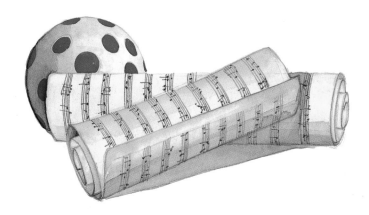

Chapter 2
Inspiration From the Ballet

In 1846, Tchaikovsky's family moved to St. Petersburg, the capital of Russia. One day, Tchaikovsky's mother took him to the theater for a ballet performance. Tchaikovsky watched while, in the darkness of the theater, a group of dancers glided across the stage. After that, whenever Tchaikovsky composed scores for ballet, images of graceful dancers inspired his music.

In 1854, when Tchaikovksy was just 14, his mother died. The loss was especially difficult for Tchaikovsky because he was away at school at the time, and he did not have a chance to say goodbye.

Chapter 3
Life in St. Petersburg

When Tchaikovsky was a teenager, he studied law to please his father. After graduating from law school, he worked for the Ministry of Justice though music continued to be his first love.

He continued composing songs and taking music lessons. He decided to leave his position at the Ministry of the Justice to pursue music seriously. He studied composition and singing at the Russian Music Society. In 1862, he enrolled at the St. Petersburg Conservatory, a school founded by Anton Rubinstein, an accomplished Russian pianist and composer.

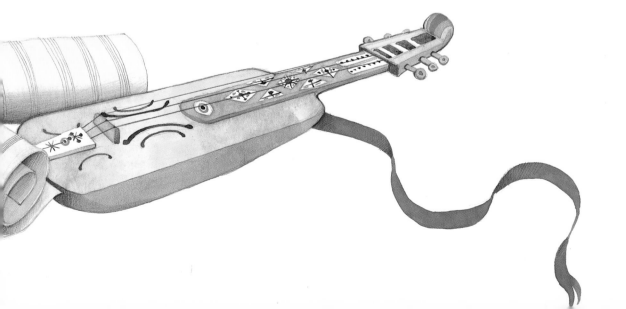

Tchaikovsky graduated with a bachelor's degree in music in 1865, at the age of 25. One of his classmates, Herman Laroche, marked the occasion by telling him, "You are the greatest musical talent in present-day Russia....I see in you the greatest, or, better said, the sole hope of our musical future."

After graduation, Tchaikovsky visited his married sister. She lived in the country in a village called Kamenka. There, Tchaikovsky enjoyed the forests and the countryside. The beauty of the landscape inspired him. He translated what he felt into his music.

Upon his return to Moscow, Tchaikovsky
was offered a position as a music theory
teacher at the newly opened Moscow
Conservatory. The dean of the school was
Anton Rubinstein's younger brother, Nicholas.
Nicholas offered to share his home with
Tchaikovsky.

During his years at the conservatory,
Tchaikovsky was able to concentrate on the
things that were the most important to him—
work, reading, and composing.

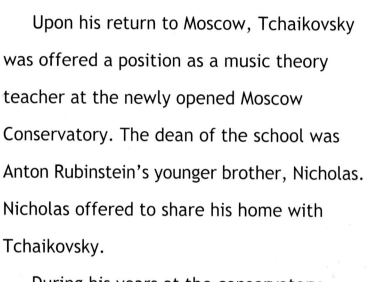

Chapter 4
Composer and Conductor

*T*chaikovsky began to be known as an extremely talented composer. Many of his musical pieces were strongly influenced by traditional folk music of Russia. While he was interested in visiting cities throughout Europe, he was always drawn back to Russia.

In 1870, when he was nearly 30 years old, Tchaikovsky began to conduct performances of his own works. As a conductor, Tchaikovsky acted nervous. He dreaded facing an orchestra and performing in front of an audience. He was often so anxious that he could not remember any of the music. Even so, he became well-known for his conducting and his composing.

Chapter 5
The Competition of 1874

*T*chaikovsky composed several kinds of musical works, including scores for the famous Russian ballet company, The Bolshoi Ballet. His work became more popular, but he was experiencing financial problems.

In 1874, he took part in a music competition. The competition required participants to create a piece based on a work by a Russian author.

Tchaikovsky mistakenly believed the deadline was in the summer of that year. With a burst of energy, he set to work. He finished the opera, *Vakula the Smith*, in only two months. Even though he created the work quickly, it was awarded first place when the contest ended in 1875.

Vakula the Smith is based on a story called *Christmas Eve*, written by Russian author, Nikolai Gogol. This complicated tale is about a man named Vakula and his love for Oksana. Vakula survives a struggle with the devil and at dawn on Christmas Day, Oksana finally agrees to marry Vakula.

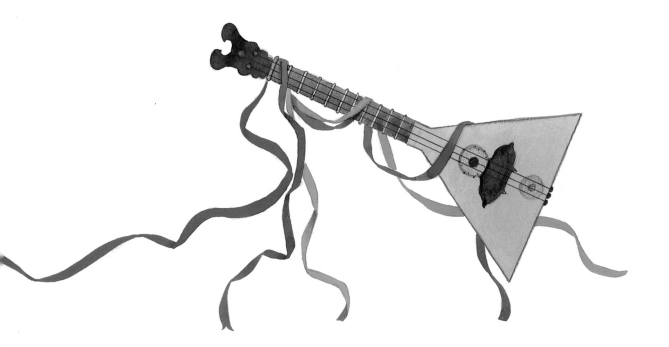

Chapter 6
A Friend and Admirer

By this time, Nadezhda von Meck, a wealthy widow, had become a great follower of Tchaikovsky's music.

She wrote to him and offered to assist him financially so that he could work on new compositions. She promised to provide him with a regular amount of money so he could maintain a certain standard of living. The only requirement was that he would continue to compose music.

Tchaikovsky accepted her offer. The two developed a special friendship, communicating both through letters and music.

Chapter 7
Marriage and Regret

*I*n 1877, Tchaikovsky met a woman named Antonina Ivanova Milyukova, and thought he was in love with her. They didn't spend much time getting to know each other before they were married.

Soon after, Tchaikovsky discovered that marriage was not for him. He knew that he could not live with someone he did not love. They separated after two months, but were

never divorced. He set out to travel around Europe in hopes of forgetting his mistake and to escape the gossip surrounding him in Russia.

Tchaikovsky stayed away from his homeland for almost a year. When he returned, he bought a house in Kamenka. He hoped that this new home in the country would help him feel happier and allow him to return to composing music.

Tchaikovsky was becoming increasingly popular. His works were being performed not only in Russia, but also throughout Europe and America. In 1891, he traveled to the United States to conduct performances of his works in several cities. One of his concerts was held at the newly opened Carnegie Hall, in New York City.

When he returned to Russia, he found that his compositions were receiving widespread acclaim and popularity. It was not long before he was recognized as one of the world's greatest contemporary composers. Tchaikovsky went to England to receive an honorary doctorate of music from Cambridge. This high award was given only to the most respected musicians and composers.

Chapter 8
The Great Contemporary Composer

*I*n 1892, Tchaikovsky's famous ballet, *The Nutcracker*, premiered in St. Petersburg. *The Nutcracker* is a story about a young girl named Clara, who receives a nutcracker shaped as a soldier from her beloved godfather, Drosselmeier, on Christmas Eve. That night, Clara has a dream about being kidnapped by the Mouse King and rescued by the nutcracker, which has been transformed into a prince. This ballet is still popular today, with performances worldwide during the Christmas season.

By 1893, though Tchaikovsky had become famous throughout the world, he still suffered from periods of deep sadness. Composing and playing music seemed to be the only activity that made him feel better.

That same year, Tchaikovsky created his last symphony, the *Pathétique*. This symphony seemed to express his sadness.

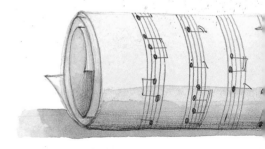

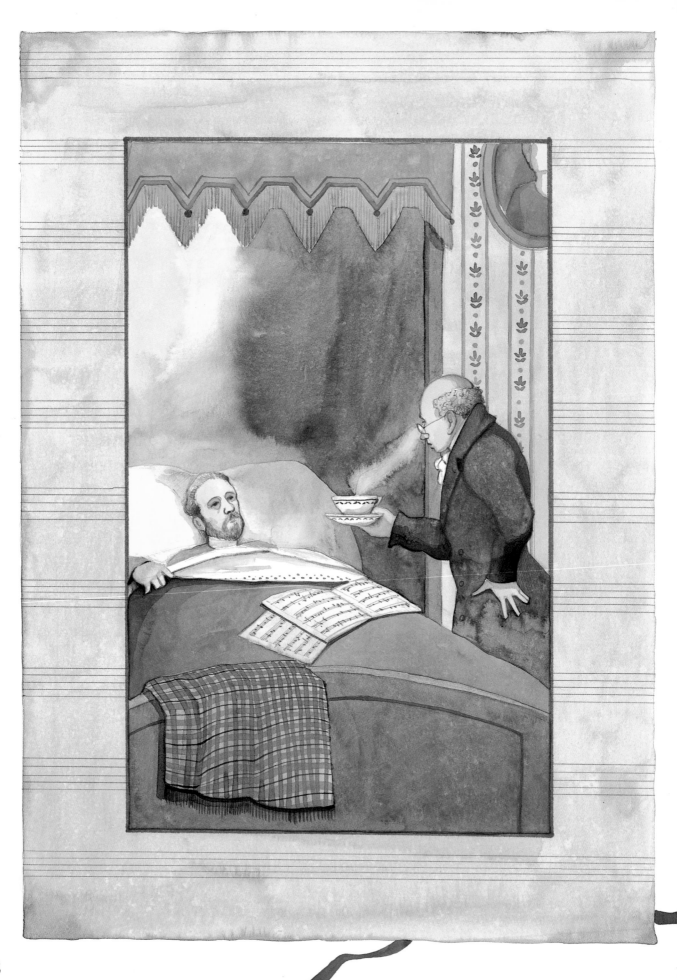

Chapter 9
One Final Performance

In November of 1893, Tchaikovsky became ill with cholera, the same disease that had killed his mother. His family took care of him, but his condition worsened.

Peter Ilich Tchaikovsky died on November 6, 1893, just nine days after the first performance of *Pathétique*. This moving and rich symphony was his final goodbye.

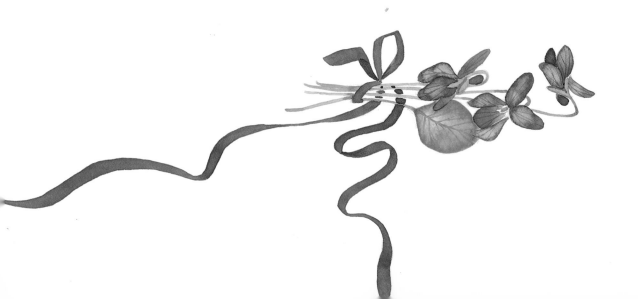

Introduction to Ballet

$\mathcal{T}$chaikovsky wrote several ballets, including *The Nutcracker*, *Swan Lake*, and *The Sleeping Beauty*. Ballet is a theatrical form of dance, accompanied by music. Through music and movement, ballet tells stories, expresses feelings, and shows the beauty of dance.

Ballet began in Italy in the 14th — 17th centuries, during a period called the Renaissance. At that time, ballet was performed for only the members of royal families. The earliest true ballet is known as *Ballet Comique de la Reine*, which was first performed in Paris, France, in 1581. Because ballet was more fully developed in France, ballet terms are usually in the French language.

Ballet movements are based on five basic positions of the feet. Because ballet requires enormous skill and strength, professional ballet dancers usually begin their training when they are quite young. Ballet dancers must be in top physical condition so that they can interpret the music and the story of the ballet through dance.